HURRICANE

in action

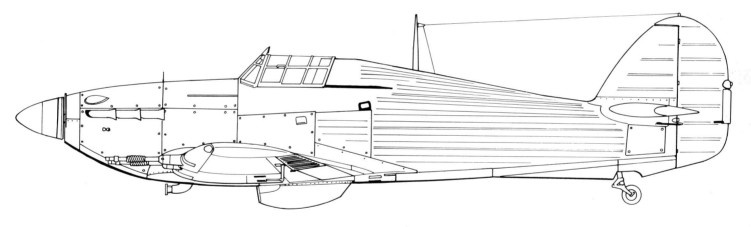

by Jerry Scutts

color illustrations by Don Greer

squadron/signal publications

Hurricane Mk IIA of No 615 (County of London) Squadron during April of 1941 in a 'B' scheme. The machine was a gift aircraft purchased by Croydon the name and crest of which appear in the 'K' of the Squadron code letters.

ISBN 0-89747-174-1

If you have any photographs of the aircraft, armor, soldiers or ships of any nation, particularly wartime snapshots, why not share them with us and help make Squadron/Signal's books all the more interesting and complete in the future. Any photograph sent to us will be copied and the original returned. The donor will be fully credited for any photos used. Please indicate if you wish us not to return the photos. Please send them to: Squadron/Signal Publications, Inc., 1115 Crowley Dr., Carrollton, TX 75011-5010.

The author would like to thank the following individuals and organizations for supplying photographs for this volume:

Chris Shores

Bruce Robertson

Dick Ward

Ron Mackay

Public Archives of Canada

Imperial War Museum

Gen Sikorsky Historical Institute

Howard Levy

Mike Stroud and Garry Lillistone

British Aerospace Kingston

Gordon Dare, BAe Kingston

Ministry of Defense (RAF)

Frantisek Sazel

A 'Vic' of three Mk Is fly over another Hurricane of No 242 Squadron in April of 1941.

3

INTRODUCTION

The logical outcome of a long line of classic biplanes built by Hawker Aircraft Limited, the Hurricane is assured a place in the *Aviation Hall Of Fame* as the first monoplane fighter to enter service with the Royal Air Force, and the first British fighter to exceed 300 mph in level flight. Rugged and reliable, it was numerically the most important aircraft in RAF inventory during the early years of World War II and went on to serve throughout the conflict in every combat theater.

The Hawker company was fortunate in having the brilliant talents of Sydney Camm, who had been appointed Chief Designer of the H G Hawker Engineering Company, the forerunner of Hawker Aircraft Limited, in 1925. That same year Camm designed a monoplane fighter and while it was not built, Camm, realizing that the biplane had reached its design zenith, continued to investigate the monoplane which he felt would be the interceptor of the future. In 1933, under Camm's direction, the Hawker design team began work on a monoplane with informal design proposals being made to the Air Ministry in August of 1935. These proposals were basically a monoplane adaption of the very successful Hawker Fury biplane powered by a 660 hp Rolls-Royce Goshawk steam cooled engine and was known as the Fury Monoplane.

However, far greater performance potential was foreseen by installation of the PV 12, another Rolls-Royce engine that would ultimately evolve into the famous line of Merlin engines. Camm drew up a monoplane based on this powerplant, incorporating a wide track hand operated retractable landing gear with low pressure tires, a retracting tail wheel, and an enclosed cockpit. The new design was based on the Air Ministry Specification F.5/34, but in August of 1934 a new requirement was formulated around Camm's own design under Specification F.36/34.

Known simply as the *Interceptor Monoplane*, this proposal was submitted on 4 September 1934 and in the closing months of the year Hawker began work on a mock-up. At this stage the aircraft was to be armed with only four guns. This appeared to Camm to be a step backward, especially since the earlier F.5/34 specification had stipulated eight guns. Work proceeded on the assumption of a four-gun armament, a Vickers mounted in each side of the fuselage with a single Vickers or Browning being mounted in each wing. Official approval for construction of a prototype was given on 21 February 1935 with a military serial of K5083.

While the Interceptor Monoplane had a number of advanced features, the new aircraft basically employed traditional Hawker biplane construction of tubular metal cross-braced sections with fabric covering. While prototype construction was underway Specification F.36/34 was changed to include a wing armament of eight license built American .303 Browning machine guns.

Power was provided by a twelve cylinder Merlin 'C' engine (the eleventh example built) of 1,029 hp driving a Watts two bladed fixed pitch wooden propeller. Despite early teething troubles with the newly developed Rolls-Royce engine, the performance of the Hurricane prototype projected excellent potential, including a maximum sea level speed of 290 mph, a maximum speed of 312 mph at 20,000 ft, a ceiling of 33,600 ft and a range of 525 miles.

On 23 October the prototype was taken from the Canbury Park Road facility to the Hawker assembly shed at Brooklands for final assembly. With Chief Test Pilot PWS 'George' Bulman at the controls K5083 lifted into the air for the first time on 6 November 1935.

The prototype spent some four months undergoing manufacturer's trials with a number of improvements being made. The canopy hood panels were strengthened to solve a vibration problem in the hood, a larger radiator and fairing were installed to solve a heating problem, and the temporary tailplane strut was removed and a trim tab was added to the rudder. In February of 1936 K5083 was delivered to the Aeroplane & Armament Experimental Establishment (A&AEE) at Martlesham Heath, Suffolk, for initial service handling tests which were conducted between 18 and 24 February. And while generally enthusiastic about the aircraft, A&AEE pilots recommended modification to the canopy to prevent it from locking shut at speeds above 150 mph and attention being paid to the lower mainwheel covers, which folded outward when the machine was parked. These covers were subsequently removed. A completely revised windscreen and canopy were installed.

However the most adverse criticism was levelled at the engine, which suffered various failures. Merlin engines 15, 17 and 19 'off the line' were installed in turn, but the failures continued. Carburetion

(Below) Prototype K5083 on an early flight still equipped with the original 'scalloped' lower edge to the windscreen but with the additional bracing on the hood to reduce vibration. Without paint the difference between fabric and metal skinning can be easily seen.

Hurricane Prototype (Early)

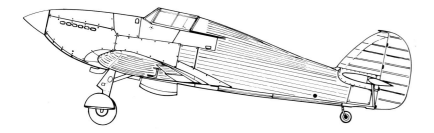

particularly was cause for concern, but generally Martlesham test pilots liked K5083's lack of inherent vices and reported that it was easy to fly.

Merlin engine development led to the 'C' series being abandoned in favor of the 'F' series for production as the Merlin I. This in turn would soon be replaced by the 'G' or Merlin II as it was designated. However, the engine which was to power most of the initial production Hurricanes would be the further refined Merlin III of 1,030 hp.

While prototype evaluation continued, Hawker received the first production order under a contract placed on 3 June 1936, for six hundred aircraft, the largest production order ever placed for a single military aircraft type during peacetime. The name *Hurricane* was officially approved on the 27th of the same month. The prototype would serve as a test aircraft until the last year of peace when it became an instructional airframe.

(Below)The main features of the prototype can be seen, which include outward hinged landing gear covers, an unfaired retractable tail wheel and short six exhaust stubs. The revised windscreen has been fitted for service trials and the tail plane brace has been removed. (Bruce Robertson)

DEVELOPMENT

Hurricane Prototype (Late)

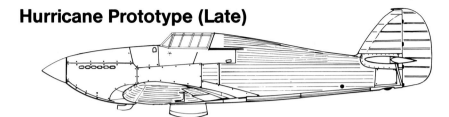

Hurricane Mk I (Early)

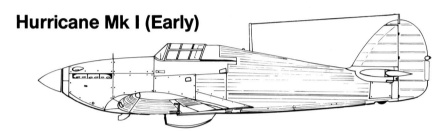

Hurricane Mk I (Late)

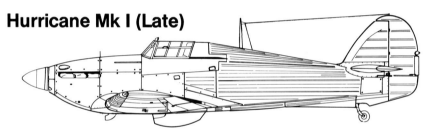

Hurricane Mk IIB

Hurricane Mk IIC

Hurricane Mk IID

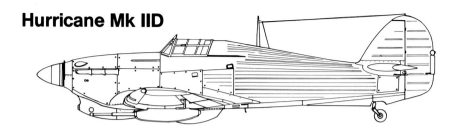

Hurricane Mk IV

Hurricane Mk V

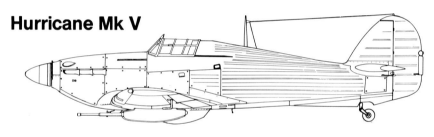

Sea Hurricane Mk IIC

Hurricane Mk X

HURRICANE MK I

Installation of the new Rolls Royce Merlin II powerplant, with its change in inclination of the rocker box flanges and consequent redesign of the upper engine cowling contour caused a delay in production of the Hurricane. Alterations to the upper engine cowling shape required the glycol header tank to be repositioned and new mountings installed. The carburetor air intake was shortened, the airscrew reduction gear ratio was increased some forty rpms for take-off and the airscrew pitch was decreased a half degree on the standard Watts Type Z.38 two bladed wooden propeller. The radiator was lengthened, and buried in the fabric covered wings were eight .303 (modified from American 30 caliber) Browning machine guns harmonized to converge at 650 yards. Landing lights were installed in the leading edge of each wing outboard of the machine guns. The first production Hurricane Mk I (L1547) with an 'all up weight' of 5,459 pounds, was flown for the first time on 12 October 1937 with Phillip Lucas at the controls. Built to Specification 15/36, the aircraft was sent to Martlesham Heath for evaluation.

By the fall of 1937 the Hurricane was in full production. These early aircraft were similar to the prototype with several minor modifications, three kidney shaped exhaust pipes replaced the six exhaust stubs on each side of the cowling, and the landing gear doors were redesigned with the outward folding lower covers being deleted. The nose contours were further refined and a post for the ring and bead sight was added. The windscreen was now a frameless molding with an optically flat panel in front of the pilot. The tailwheel, fully retractable on K5083, was fixed in the down position. The airframe, mainly fabric covered, lacked any armor plate.

By November enough Mk Is had been built to equip one flight of No 111 (Fighter) Squadron at Northolt, who spent the early months of 1938 'breaking in' the new fighter. By March of 1938 produc-

(Above) The camouflage and markings are very evident on this near pristine early production Hurricane Mk I (L1582), which carries radio antenna masts on the fuselage and tail fin. A 'bead' sight has been installed on the nose and the internal optically flat panel has been added to the windscreen. (Robertson)

(Below) The first production Hurricane Mk I (L1547) with the revised 'kidney' shaped exhaust stacks and external instrument venturi mounted on the fuselage just below the windscreen. The engine change caused a small fairing to be added to the cowling just above the front exhaust. Ortho film has reversed the roundel colors and almost obliterated the serial number on the rear fuselage. (Hawker Aircraft)

(Above) Under evaluation by Yugoslavia during 1938, this Mk I has the distinctive nose contours of the very early Hurricane, and one of the earliest modifications to the Hurricane Mk I, the six inch extension to the rudder and the addition of fairings added fore and aft of the tail wheel which has been made non-retractable. (Robertson)

(Above Left) Another of the numerous small changes made to the Mk I was the addition of pull-back handles on the outside of the cockpit canopy. A starter crank is in position just in front of the wing leading edge. This machine carries the half Black underwing finish seen on aircraft during the early part of the war. (Robertson)

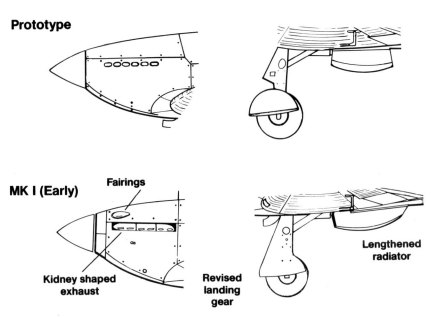

Prototype

MK I (Early)

Fairings

Kidney shaped exhaust

Revised landing gear

Lengthened radiator

(Below Left) An early Mk I of No 56 Squadron prior to September of 1939, when the code letters were changed to 'US'. (Robertson)

(Above) Riggers and fitters learn the intricacies of modern RAF aircraft at a technical training school in the Midlands, circa 1939. This early Hurricane production carcass appears to have the chalked-on fin serial no 1357M, the 'M' denoting that the aircraft was intended only for ground instruction. (Robertson)

(Above Right) This ground crew takes a break during lifting operations to get a Mk I (believed to be L2039) out of the way at Tangmere. Belonging to No 501 Squadron, it carries a squadron leader's pennant on the fin. (R L Ward)

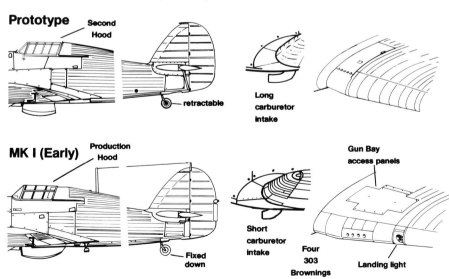

Prototype — Second Hood — retractable — Long carburetor intake

MK I (Early) — Production Hood — Fixed down — Short carburetor intake — Four 303 Brownings — Gun Bay access panels — Landing light

(Below, Right) A Mk I of No 1 Squadron of the South African Air Force (SAAF) at Port Reitz in June of 1940. No 1 was the first SAAF squadron to receive Hurricanes. (Via Chris Shores).

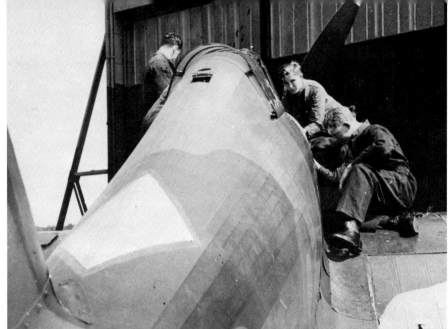

(Above) An unusual view of a Hurricane Mk I showing the diamond gas detection patch forward of the fin and the radio mast and dorsal identification light locations aft of the cockpit.

tion had reached six aircraft per week and No 3 Squadron began receiving Hurricane Is concurrent with additional changes on the production lines. Spin tests at Martlesham and RAE Farnborough had revealed a shielding effect on the rudder. To correct this problem the rudder was extended three inches and a ventral fairing was added fore and aft of the tailwheel which considerably improved the airflow at the base of the rudder. Tests by night — and day — indicated an exhaust glare problem and a horizontal shield was recommended for both sides of the fuselage to reduce it. A further modification was also made to the exhaust system with Rolls Royce ejector exhaust pipes replacing the kidney shaped exhaust pipes with a resulting increase in speed of two miles per hour.

Hurricane Mk I Late Production

With Mk I production well underway, the company continued work on a metal skinned wing for the Hurricane. One had been built at Kingston toward the end of 1938 and flight-tested for the first time on 28 April 1939. Production Hurricanes began to receive metal skinned wings later in the year with many original Mk Is being retro-fitted with them during overhauls.

When it became known that Germany's Messerschmitt Bf 109 was being armed with 20MM cannons, work was begun on adding armor plating to the Hurricane. An armoured windscreen was added and an armored bulkhead was installed immediately in front of the cockpit. Plans were made to add armour plating aft of the pilot seat.

The early Hurricane was equipped with Watts two bladed wooden propellers for some months but in January of 1939 Hurricanes equipped with de Havilland Hamilton three bladed two-pitch propellers began to reach service units (No 213 Squadron) and by the outbreak of war most Hurricanes in squadron service were equipped with either de Havilland or Rotol three-bladed constant speed propellers.

The Merlin III with a standardized shaft capable of accepting either the de Havilland Hamilton or the Rotol propeller was introduced during construction of the second batch of 300 Mk Is, as were the metal-covered wings and external bullet-proof windscreens.

(Above) Removal of the port fuselage metal panels shows the mass of structural tubing and controls on the port side of the cockpit — the Hurricane had no inner cockpit wall or floor — the seat, instrument panel and controls being attached to the basic tubular super-structure. No squadron carried the code on the side of this Hurricane and the machine is believed to have been part of the Horsham St Faith Station Flight, aircraft of which were coded 'GD'. (Hawker)

(Above) Another 'prang', this time a Mk I of No 232 Squadron which was en route from Manston to Croydon on 10 September 1939 with Sgt Alec Butterick at the controls. The dismantling job is well under way, the guns having been removed for safety. (R L Ward)

(Above) Some of the first Hurricanes to go into combat were the Mk Is of the Belgian Air Force. This early Mk I was badly shot up while attacking an intruding Dornier Do 17 on 3 May 1940, but made it back to base, whereas two other attacking Hurricanes did not.

OVERSEAS ORDERS

As Hurricanes reached RAF squadrons in increasing numbers, Hawker fulfilled export orders for the type. Even as the clouds of war darkened some one hundred Hurricanes were exported to the Air Forces of Allies.

The first foreign country to evaluate the Hurricane was Yugoslavia, which had previously purchased and license built earlier Hawker aircraft. A single Hurricane Mk I taken from RAF production orders, was delivered to Yugoslavia in December of 1938 for evaluation. After flight tests in Belgrade an order for twelve Hurricanes was placed, followed by a second order of twelve in February of 1940. In the meantime, a production license had been negotiated with plans to build forty Hurricanes at the the PSFAZ Rogozarski plant in Belgrade, another sixty at the state factory at Zmaj. By early April of 1941 the Royal Yugoslav Air Force had some forty-eight Hurricanes on strength, about half of them home-built examples. Equipping fighter squadrons in three fighter regiments they saw constant action in the week following the German invasion of Yugoslavia on 6 April 1941, making interceptions over Zagreb and Bosnia, as well as carrying out ground attacks on advancing German columns. These stopped on 13 April due to the speed of the German advance, the intention being to evacuate surviving aircraft to Greece. However, only a few managed to get away, as fog prevented most remaining Yugoslav aircraft from taking off and they had to be destroyed on the ground by their crews. Unfortunately a similar fate overtook the handful of aircraft that did reach Greece, with German bombs making short work of them at Paramythia airfield. One of two examples in the fighter school at Mostar was captured by the Italians.

In an attempt to bolster Poland's defenses with more modern aircraft in the face of German saber rattling ten Mk Is were shipped to the Polish Air Force. These aircraft were en route as Hitler launched his attack into Poland on the morning of 1 September 1939. Only the evaluation machine (L2048) had been delivered to Poland before the German blow fell. Those aircraft enroute were diverted to the RAF at Gibralter.

Also in transit at the outbreak of hostilities were twelve Hurricanes enroute to Rumania. And while

(Below) One of the twelve Hurricanes shipped to Rumania just before hostilities broke out.

(Above) Late production Mk Is of No 111 Squadron being fuelled from an Albion bowser at Wick, Scotland, in February of 1940, when the unit was providing air cover for shipping in Scapa Flow. (IWM)

they were delivered it is not known if they saw action.

Turkey took delivery of fifteen Hurricane Mk Is contracted for, with deliveries being made during the first two months after the outbreak of war. Neighboring Persia (Iran) took delivery of a single Hurricane in 1939 (L2079), followed by one (P3270) in 1940.

The South African Air Force (SAAF) would use substantial quantities of Hurricanes. The first three (L1708, L1710 and L1711) were shipped to Durban for final assembly in December of 1938, and issued to No 1 Squadron at Pretoria, which would be among the Allied fighter units to use the Mk I during the early campaigns in the Western Desert. No 1 (SAAF) Squadron, along with its sister squadrons, Nos 2 (SAAF) and 3 (SAAF) were instrumental in completely overcoming Italian opposition in Ethiopia before the focus of attention turned to challenging the Luftwaffe.

Among the first Hurricanes to see combat were the Mk Is operated by the Belgian Air Force. Early in 1939 twenty Mk Is had been sold to Belgium with the intention for Avions Fairey (*Societe Anonyme Belge*) to build a further eighty under license. Only two Belgian built examples, both fitted with four 12.65мм machine guns in place of the .303 Brownings, were completed before 10 May 1940, when Belgium was invaded. As early as 3 May the Belgians lost three Hurricanes to enemy aircraft and on the fateful 10th of May only eleven British-built machines remained, equipping *Groupe 1/2 Le Chardon* (The Thistle). Nine of them were destroyed in the early attack on Schaffen, with the remaining two aircraft being repairable given time. But there was no time and Belgium joined the subjugated countries of Europe.

Finland was sold twelve ex-RAF Hurricane Is after the signing of the Winter War Armistice on 13 March 1940 ending the Russian invasion of Finland. Only eleven Hurricanes arrived, one being lost en route. Issued to fighter squadron *HLeLv 30*, these Hurricanes operated in flight strength alongside a flight of Dutch built Fokker D.XXIs in the Continuation War against Russia. Attrition whittled the number of Hurricanes to one by the time hostilities ceased in 1945.

(Above) No 85 Squadron's distinctive hexagon insignia is carried on the fin of a late production Mk I VY-C in France during May of 1940. Armorers in the foreground are making up belts of .303 ammunition. This machine has been fitted with a de Havilland Hamilton three bladed two pitch propeller. (Bruce Robertson).

Hurricane Wings

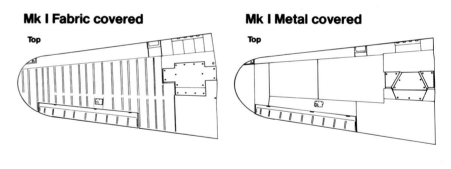

Mk I Fabric covered
Top

Bottom

Mk I Metal covered
Top

Bottom

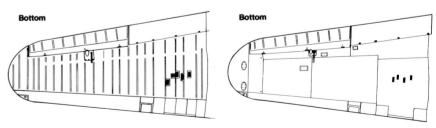

(Below Left) An overhaul for late production Mk I P3886/UF-K of No 601 (County of London) Squadron at Tangmere under less than ideal conditions during early 1940. Partially repainted, the aircraft retains Black fuselage undersides and has a factory applied fin flash with 9 inch Blue and White stripes, with the rest of the fin painted Red. (IWM)

(Above) Late production Hurricane Mk I KW-U of 615 Squadron brought down in France.

Propeller Development

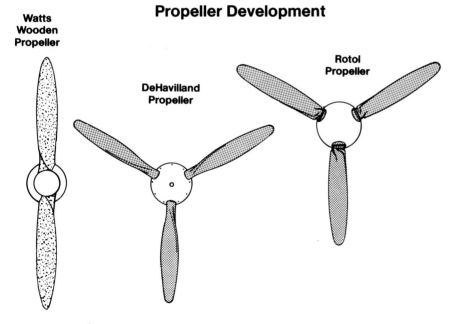

Watts Wooden Propeller

DeHavilland Propeller

Rotol Propeller

(Below Right) This multi-color underside finish was carried on Hurricanes as a quick identification from the summer of 1938 to June of 1940. There were many variations to the scheme seen — a White starboard wing, Black port wing, with the rest of the undersides painted aluminum.

(Above) Late production Hurricane Mk Is, including P3733, aboard the carrier HMS ARGUS while enroute to Malta in August of 1940. On arrival at Luqa these machines of No 418 Flight were formed into No 261 Squadron. (Shores)

Other users of the Mk I included Egypt, which used a small number for the defense of Cairo in 1941, and Ireland, where the Irish Air Corps purchased an example which made a forced-landing in Eire. A dozen more were subsequently purchased.

RAF Service

Being the most numerous modern British fighter available, the Hurricane quickly entered service with RAF squadrons around the world — although in some areas even substantial numbers proved to be too little, too late. This was particularly so in the Far East where the Hawker fighter was a Godsend to squadrons which would have otherwise been flying antiquated biplanes or obsolete monoplanes such as the Brewster Buffalo which could offer only token resistance to the Japanese Mitsubishi A6M Zero.

Hurricane Mk Is were active in the defense of Singapore and the subsequent fighting in Sumatra and Java and although the overall RAF effort achieved little, the Hurricane made its mark. It was to become the principal British fighter-bomber in that theater virtually until the end of the war, the early marks being supplanted by later variants before the Japanese were finally beaten.

With war clouds gathering over Europe it was an obvious move for Hawker to set up additional sources of Hurricane production in the event of the Hawker facilities being bombed. Spare capacity was

available at the Gloster Aircraft plant at Hucclecote/Brockworth in Gloucestershire, Hawker having purchased this company in 1934. A new production plant was laid down in 1938 and an initial production batch of 500 Hurricanes begun prior to the outbreak of war. The first Hurricane Mk I (L2020), was rolled out on 27 October 1939. By the end of 1940 the Gloster facility had turned out 1,211 Hurricanes and another 1,359 by the close of 1941. Gloster production ceased in March of 1942 after a grand total of 2,750 airframes had been completed in four separate batches.

Since it was a distinct possibility that any British factory could be destroyed or severely damaged by the enemy if and when war came, Hawker arranged to have Hurricanes license built in Canada. Following negotiations with the Canadian Car & Foundry Co (CC&F) a contract was signed for an initial batch of forty Mk Is to be built at the Fort William plant in Ontario. CC&F's first Hurricane (P5170) was flown on 10 January 1940. Outwardly similar to British Mk Is Canadian Hurricanes had metal-skinned wings and the majority were powered by American Packard-built Merlins. Initial machines with Rolls-Royce Merlins driving de Havilland propellers were shipped to the UK complete, but subsequent deliveries were without engines, armament and instruments with final assembly being made in the UK.

After 166 Mk Is had been built in Canada, production was switched to the Hurricane Mk X, the designation used to identify Hurricanes powered by American manufactured Packard Merlin 28 engines. Ten of the Canadian built Mk Is were lost in transit, with the balance arriving in England in time to participate in the Battle of Britain, examples going to RAF squadrons on an as required basis.

By the outbreak of war the RAF had 497 Mk I Hurricanes on strength, enough to fully equip eighteen squadrons. Four of these, Nos 1, 73, 85 and 87, joined the Air Component of the British Expeditionary Force, which had begun moving to France on 15 September 1939. After establishing themselves in France Hurricanes flew reconnaissance patrols along the German border during the 'Phoney War' having occasional brushes with the enemy. No 1 Squadron's first kill was a Dornier Do 17, shot down near Toul on 30 October 1939.

In January of 1940 RAF squadrons in France were reorganized as British Air Forces in France, which co-ordinated the operations of the Air Component and the Advanced Air Striking Force. When the German attack on the West came on 10 May 1940 three additional Hurricane units, Nos 3, 79 and 504 Squadrons, were quickly dispatched from England.

These precious machines could hardly be spared from home defense, British air chiefs realizing that if things went badly in France an air assault on England would inevitably follow. These fears were well-founded as the Germans swept through France; the decimation of the British squadrons on the continent included the loss of 72 Hurricanes and 120 damaged -- a grim total of nearly 200 invaluable fighters were lost since the damaged aircraft had to be left behind when there was no time to ship them across the Channel.

Radio Masts

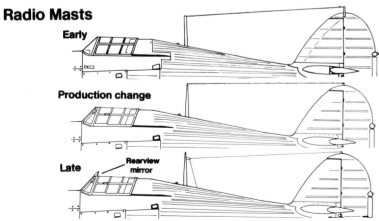

Early

Production change

Late — Rearview mirror

(Below Right) Early production Mk Is (L2101 and L2067) retrofitted with three bladed propellers standing among later production Hurricanes at a repair depot in 1940. Early Mk Is were usually brought up to late Mk I standards during major repairs. (Robertson)

(Above) Not a new aircraft production line, but the all-important repair of damaged Hurricanes at the Kingston plant. Identifiable Mk Is are V7100, V7246, Z3671 and V6857. A variety of fuselage markings on aircraft in the background include full squadron codes and Sky fuselage bands. (Hawker)

(Above) Port side of V7118 of No. 306 Torunski (City of Torun) Squadron at RAF Church Fenton or Tern Hill in November of 1940. Proudly displaying their national insignia on virtually every aircraft they flew while with the RAF or USAAF, Polish pilots often decorated their machines with the badges of their original Polish Air Force squadrons, as can be seen by the wild duck painted on a White diamond emblem aft of the exhaust. (IWM)

(Below Left) Starboard side of the (above) aircraft showing the similar location of the Polish Air Force insignia and squadron badge, as well as variations in application of the code letters. (Gen Sikorsky Historical Institute)

Herculean efforts by both factories and RAF conversion and training units nevertheless boosted the number of Hurricane squadrons to twenty-six before the Luftwaffe's main attack on the British Isles. However, three of these were only partially equipped and four others were in the process of working-up after having lost their aircraft and equipment in France. These Hurricane squadrons, along with nineteen Spitfire squadrons and ten other fighter squadrons mostly equipped with Defiants and Blenheims, met German bombing raids on the Channel ports, the vital chain of radio direction finding stations, airfields, towns and cities throughout the summer of 1940. During the first major challenge, a challenge by a modern well equipped and trained air force, that the *Luftwaffe* had had to face in WWII. The battle for air superiority over England saw RAF Fighter Command marshal its two main fighter types, Hurricanes and Spitfires, into four groups, concentrating them to best meet the *Luftwaffe* attack, with Hurricanes mainly attacking the bombers and Spitfires concentrating on the fighters. When Hurricanes met the Bf 109, the Hawker fighter was slightly outclassed in speed and armament —however they were close enough in performance that the outcome would usually depend on the training and skill of the opposing pilots. However when it sustained damage, the Hurricane's sturdy tubular construction stood it in good stead and many machines were repaired and returned to active duty.

The sheer aggressiveness of the British squadrons tended to nullify any shortcomings in the penetrating power of their rifle-caliber machine guns and it should be remembered that single seat fighters armed with eight and ten guns were still a big innovation by world standards in 1940. The sheer psychological effect of the hose piping streams of fire aimed at the rather poorly protected bombers so unnerved many German crews that they broke formation. When this happened individual Heinkel, Dornier and Junkers bombers became relatively easy meat for the defenders. Hurricane pilots found little difficulty in dealing with twin engine Messerschmitt Bf 110 fighters and the much vaunted terror weapon of the Blitzkreig, the Junkers Ju 87 Stuka.

It was while attacking a Bf 110 on 16 August 1940 that Flt Lt James Nicholson was to win the only Victoria Cross awarded to a pilot of Fighter Command during the war. On fire from an attack by a Bf 109, Nicholson's Hurricane and another of No 249 Squadron survived the German 'bounce'. Remaining at the controls long enough to shoot down a Bf 110 that had flown into his sights, Nicholson baled out. Badly burned and then wounded by defense volunteers who mistook him for a German, he survived only to be killed in action later in the war.

By the end of the daylight phase of the Battle of Britain a total of 2,648 British and German aircraft had been destroyed. The Hurricane's role had been decisive and included fifty-seven percent of all German aircraft shot down in combat. No less that 272 Bf 109s had been downed for the loss of 153 Hurricanes in combats involving just those two fighter types. Seven of the seventeen British and Allied fighter pilots who scored ten or more victories during the battle flew Hurricanes although some had also scored kills while flying the Spitfire.

Exhaust Pipes

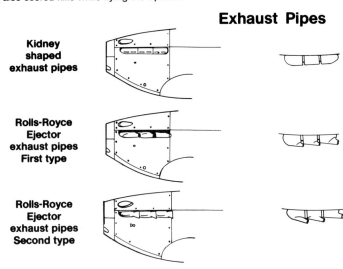

Kidney shaped exhaust pipes

Rolls-Royce Ejector exhaust pipes First type

Rolls-Royce Ejector exhaust pipes Second type

(Above) Hurricane Mk I of No 306 Squadron. The flame damper plate was widely fitted to day as well as night fighter Hurricanes. (GSHI)

(Above) A Polish armorer carefully feeds an ammunition belt to one of the Hurricane's wing guns, the open breeches of which can be seen. Replacement of the kidney shaped exhaust pipes with Rolls-Royce ejector exhaust pipes added two mph to the top speed of the Mk I.(GSHI)

(Above) During re-arming the depth of the wing at the gun bays can be seen. Some 1200 rounds were needed to fully arm each four gun battery. (GSHI)

Wing Armament

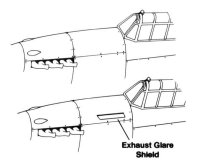

Landing Light

Four .303 Brownings

Gun Camera (some machines)

Gun openings were often covered with patches of fabric

Gun Camera

Glare Shield

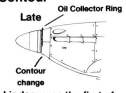

Exhaust Glare Shield

Nose Contour

Early

Late

Oil Collector Ring

Contour change

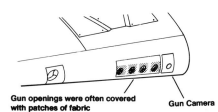

(Below Right) Enter the Eagles. No 71 (Eagle) Squadron at Kirton-in-Lindsey was the first of three squadrons manned by American volunteers. Mk I V7608 in the foreground carries a Black wing. (IWM)

At the height of the Battle of Britain in June of 1940, Britain commenced hostilities with Italy in the Middle East. In August No 274 Squadron was the first Hurricane squadron formed in the theater, with No 261 Squadron being formed on Hurricanes the same month on Malta to add a much-needed boost to the island's defense against the *Regia Aeronautica*.

Hurricanes intended for tropical and desert operations had to have their engines protected against abrasive sand and dust entering the carburetion system and late in 1939 tropical trials were undertaken with an early Mk I. With a filter faired into the underside of the nose, this aircraft was tested at Martlesham Heath, followed by an extensive series of trials in Egypt, completed in July of 1940, which confirmed that the desert filter was adequate in reducing engine wear. This distinctive fairing would become one of the most common modifications seen on wartime Hurricanes.

HURRICANE Mk I (PR)
Photo Reconnaissance

A small number of Mk I airframes formed the basis for the photo-reconnaissance Hurricanes used in the Middle and Far Eastern theaters. The first machines were locally-modified at Heliopolis, Egypt for use by the newly formed No 2 Photographic Reconnaissance Unit: serial No W9116 carried three 14 inch F.24 cameras in the lower rear fuselage (one vertical and two oblique) and V7423 and V7428, each had two 8 inch F.24s. When W9116 was lost on 3 October 1941, W9353 replaced it.

(Above) As the Nazi juggernaut knifed into Greece airfields were littered with shot up Hurricanes that had to be left behind when time ran out on repairs.

Dust Filter

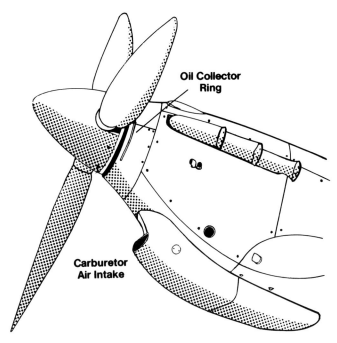

Oil Collector Ring

Carburetor Air Intake

(Below Left) Hurricanes sent to temperate climates were fitted with a faired Volkes dust filter. Tropicalization would become the most numerous modification made to the Hurricane.

17

(Above) Testing the guns of a Hurricane Mk I in Egypt during 1940. (IWM)

(Above) South African Air Force serial numbers were all-digits as seen on this Mk I of No 3 Squadron (SAAF) in March of 1941. (Shores)

(Below) Hurricane I of No 3 SAAF Squadron at Amriga, March 1941. (Shores)

(Below) An Italian style mottled camouflage was rather widely applied to Hurricanes of No 3 (SAAF) Squadron in the desert to fool enemy gunners into thinking a 'friendly' Italian fighter was approaching. This example is seen at Benina during 1941. (F F Smith va Shores)

18

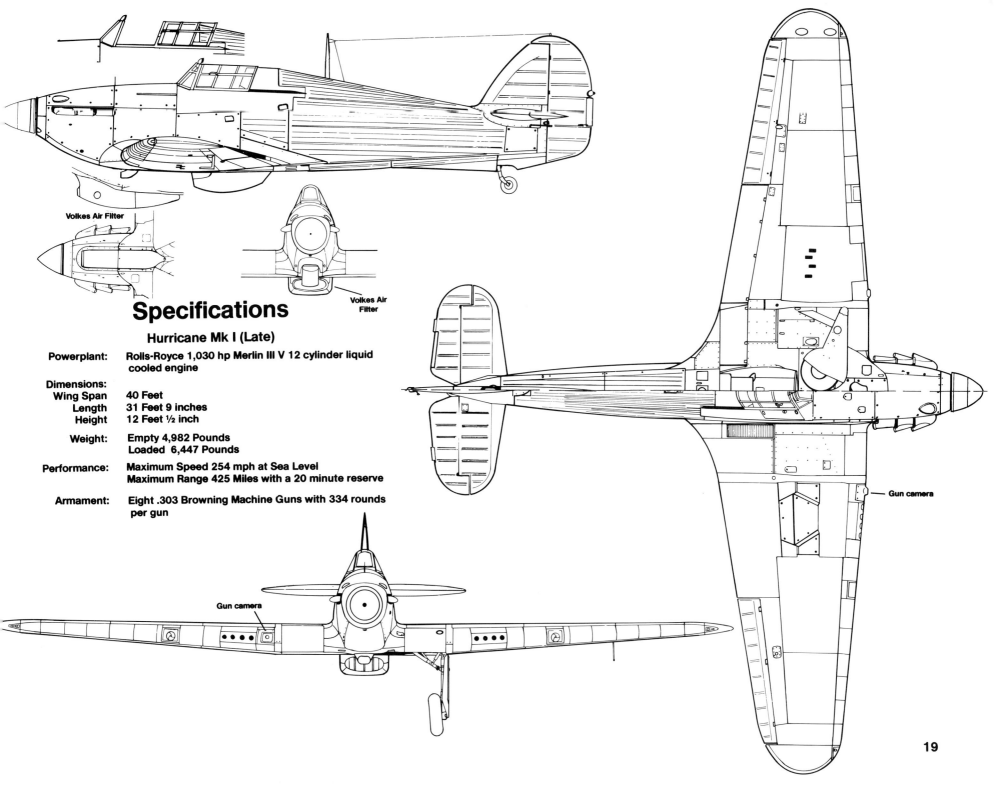

Volkes Air Filter

Volkes Air Filter

Specifications

Hurricane Mk I (Late)

Powerplant:	Rolls-Royce 1,030 hp Merlin III V 12 cylinder liquid cooled engine
Dimensions:	
Wing Span	40 Feet
Length	31 Feet 9 inches
Height	12 Feet ½ inch
Weight:	Empty 4,982 Pounds
	Loaded 6,447 Pounds
Performance:	Maximum Speed 254 mph at Sea Level
	Maximum Range 425 Miles with a 20 minute reserve
Armament:	Eight .303 Browning Machine Guns with 334 rounds per gun

Gun camera

Gun camera

19

(Above)A tactical recon Hurricane Mk I carrying the name 'Olive II' under the cockpit canopy is seen on patrol over the desert. (IWM)

(Above)Bringing them back to fight another day, RAF 'Queen Mary' trailers haul Hurricanes (including Mk I Z4603) to a desert maintenance unit.

(Below)Tropicalized Mk I at El Kabrit, Egypt in December of 1942. (Howard Levy)

(Below)This Hurricane Mk I (V7670) was captured and used by the Germans until it was liberated at Gambut in January of 1942.

(Above) This Hurricane Mk I unfortunately provides little clue to its parent unit in the desert. It is, however, believed to have been on tactical reconnaissance duties. (Via Shores)

(Above) The 'Z' prefix serial range was a large one, covering both Mk Is and Mk IIs. This Hurricane Mk I, believed to be Z4292, was on the strength of No 335 Squadron at Aqir during 1941, which was then undergoing training. This squadron was the first of two formed in the Middle East with Greek personnel. (Via Shores)

(Below) Mk I T9531 was part of the third batch of Hurricanes built for the RAF to replace those sold abroad from RAF stocks. This particular aircraft apparently saw service in the Middle East before being passed to the South African Air Force (SAAF) for training purposes. It was photographed in Rhodesia. (Robertson)

(Below) The see-saw battles in North Africa often saw airfields with salvageable aircraft that had to be left behind. On occasion they would be retrieved by advancing Allied forces.

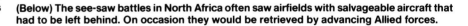

(Above) This Hurricane Mk I (V7480) was used in towed fighter experiments during 1941. Although part of a Halifax can be seen on the right, all flight trials from Staverton used Wellington 'tugs'. Originally intended to provide fighters for the defense of Malta, the experiment was an attempt to overcome the Hurricane's short range.

(Below) Another experiment to increase the Hurricane's range was to fill a second wing with fuel which would be used during a ferry flight, after which the empty wing was released. Tests were carried out with a Hurricane Mk I (L1884) modified by F Hills & Son before the scheme was abandoned.

HURRICANE MK IIA Series 1

With the daylight phase of the Battle of Britain over, the hard pressed Fighter Command squadrons were able to rest their exhausted pilots, taking delivery of new aircraft as they became available. There was at last time to introduce refinements to aircraft then in service and to look to developments for the future. But the *Luftwaffe* was by no means completely spent, particularly at night, and Hurricanes joined a miscellany of other aircraft carrying out nocturnal interception sorties as the German Night Blitz intensified during the autumn and winter of 1940. Lacking airborne interception aids most single-seaters were at a distinct disadvantage during these operations, and many sorties were abortive.

Hawker's most urgent task, however, was to improve the Hurricane's daylight performance and several alternative powerplants were considered. The choice offering the least disruption to production was the Merlin XX, which with a two-stage supercharger, and using 100 octane fuel was rated at 1,280 hp at take off. Few modifications to the fuselage were necessary to take the slightly larger engine and a seven inch fuselage bay was inserted ahead of the cockpit increasing the overall length of the Hurricane by seven inches. Hurricane I P3236 served as the Mk II prototype, flying with a Merlin XX for the first time on 11 June 1940. Top speed of the Mk II prototype was clocked at 348 mph and was the fastest Hurricane ever flown.

Production Mk II Series 1 aircraft were intended to be equipped with the new twelve gun wings, but a projected shortage of Browning machine guns meant that initial Mk IIs retained the battery of eight guns in the now standard metal skinned wings. Examples of the Hurricane Mk II Series 1 began reaching Fighter Command in September of 1940 when No 111 Squadron (the same squadron that received the first Mk Is) took delivery of the first Mk IIA srs 1s. The more powerful engine provided the early Mk II with a maximum speed of 322 mph at 13,500 feet, 342 mph at 22,000 ft and a maximum loaded weight of 7,100 pounds.

(Above) Hawker built Mk IIs belonging to No 601 (County of London) Squadron during early 1941 — shortly before the unit converted to Bell Airacobras.

(Below) A Hurricane Mk IIA Z3658/AYO-N of No 401 (Ram) Squadron RCAF at Digby, Lincs having its 1,280 hp Merlin XX engine run up by the ground crew -- the two men on the tailplane are helping to keep the rear of the aircraft on the ground during run-up — on 24 July 1941. (RCAF)

MK IIA SRS 2

Very early in the war there was found to be an almost desperate need for increasing the range of the Hurricane. Fortunately Hawker had already been conducting studies toward providing the Hurricane with under-wing auxiliary fuel tanks. The installation of attachment points and fuel lines was given the highest priority, with the first installation being made on Hurricane I P3460, flying for the first time on 7 May 1940. Initial installations were two fixed 44 (Imperial) gallon fuel tanks, which were later stressed to withstand combat maneuvers, and were in turn made jettisonable. When the Hurricane IIA Series 2 was introduced it carried universal attachment points for carrying either auxiliary fuel tanks or bombs. A degree of fuselage strengthening was necessary for the Mk II to withstand higher wing loadings. The majority of these aircraft retained the eight gun wing.

(Above)Sgt Pilot W Leadbeater of No 43 Squadron standing on the wing of a well-weathered presentation Mk II named 'Ramaekers.' (IWM)

(Below) Hurricane Mk IIAs of No 1 (SAAF) Squadron being turned into their take off position churn up a mini-sandstorm in the Western Desert. The nearest machine (5469) carries a rather crudely-painted 'S' ID letter on its fuselage. (Via Shores)

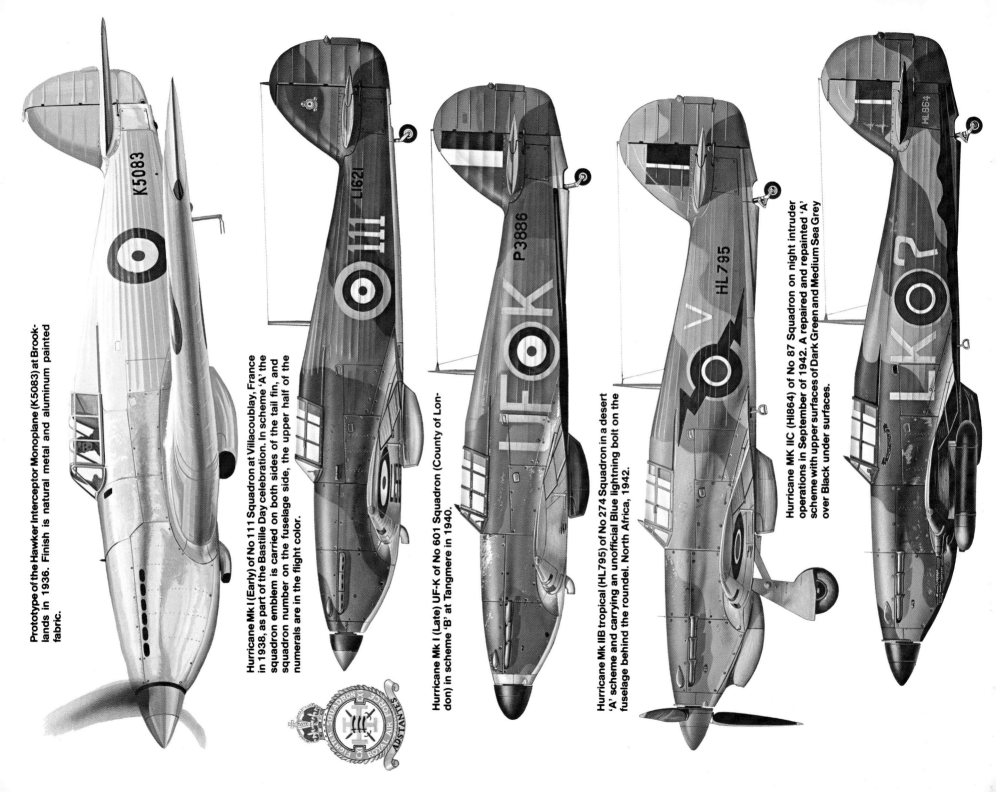

Prototype of the Hawker Interceptor Monoplane (K5083) at Brooklands in 1936. Finish is natural metal and aluminum painted fabric.

Hurricane Mk I (Early) of No 111 Squadron at Villacoublay, France in 1938, as part of the Bastille Day celebration. In scheme 'A' the squadron emblem is carried on both sides of the tail fin, and squadron number on the fuselage side, the upper half of the numerals are in the flight color.

Hurricane Mk I (Late) UF-K of No 601 Squadron (County of London) in scheme 'B' at Tangmere in 1940.

Hurricane Mk IIB tropical (HL795) of No 274 Squadron in a desert 'A' scheme and carrying an unofficial Blue lightning bolt on the fuselage behind the roundel. North Africa, 1942.

Hurricane MK IIC (HI864) of No 87 Squadron on night intruder operations in September of 1942. A repaired and repainted 'A' scheme with upper surfaces of Dark Green and Medium Sea Grey over Black under surfaces.

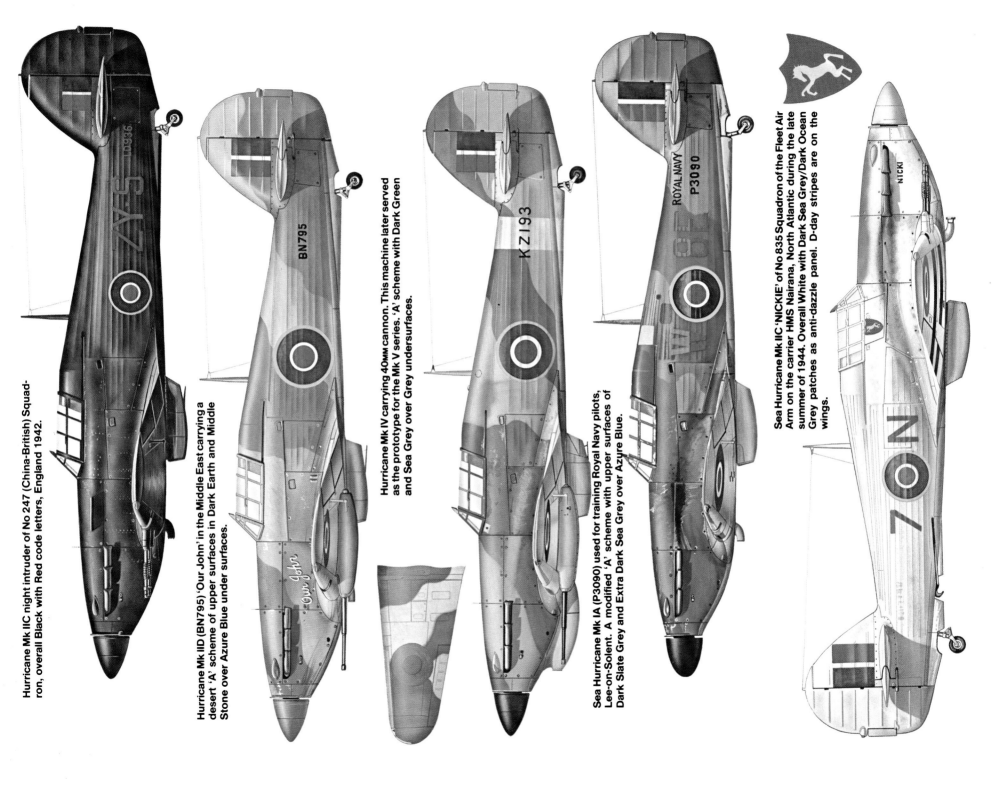

Hurricane Mk IIC night intruder of No 247 (China-British) Squadron, overall Black with Red code letters, England 1942.

Hurricane Mk IID (BN795) 'Our John' in the Middle East carrying a desert 'A' scheme of upper surfaces in Dark Earth and Middle Stone over Azure Blue under surfaces.

Hurricane Mk IV carrying 40mm cannon. This machine later served as the prototype for the Mk V series. 'A' scheme with Dark Green and Sea Grey over Grey undersurfaces.

Sea Hurricane Mk IA (P3090) used for training Royal Navy pilots, Lee-on-Solent. A modified 'A' scheme with upper surfaces of Dark Slate Grey and Extra Dark Sea Grey over Azure Blue.

Sea Hurricane Mk IIC 'NICKIE' of No 835 Squadron of the Fleet Air Arm on the carrier HMS Nairana, North Atlantic during the late summer of 1944. Overall White with Dark Sea Grey/Dark Ocean Grey patches as anti-dazzle panel. D-day stripes are on the wings.

(Above) Pilots of No 310 (Czech) Squadron run for their aircraft during 1941. No 312 flew Ramrods and Rhubarbs into France, but in November began operations against attacking German fighter-bombers. (Frantisek Sazel)

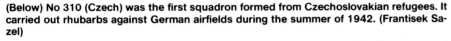

(Below) No 310 (Czech) was the first squadron formed from Czechoslovakian refugees. It carried out rhubarbs against German airfields during the summer of 1942. (Frantisek Sazel)

(Above) Pilot of No 312 (Czech) Squadron climbs aboard his Mk II. In June of 1941 312 began flying escort missions against targets along the French coast. (Frantisek Sazel)

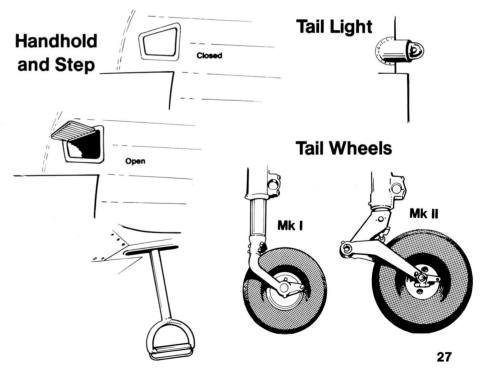

Handhold and Step

Closed

Open

Tail Light

Tail Wheels

Mk I

Mk II

27

(Above) Hurricane II under construction — the fuselage being joined to the wing center section. (Hawker)

(Above) The ladies take over to tack the fuselage fabric in place. In the background PZ795, part of the 10th and last batch of Hurricanes built in the UK, has its serial stencilled under the cockpit — as does the partially covered example in the foreground. This production batch covered both Mk IIs and IVs. (Hawker)

(Below) Easy does it. The 1,280 Merlin XX engine, heart of the Hurricane, is lowered onto the waiting stress-bearing framework. (Hawker)

(Below) Full flap travel is tested before the aircraft is rolled out. The all metal wing became standard on the late production Mk I. (Hawker)

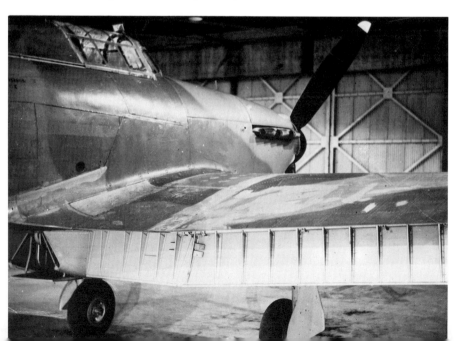

HURRICANE MK IIB
Hurri-Bomber

To provide the RAF with a fighter-bomber the wings of the Hurricane were stressed to carry a 250 pound bomb on streamlined racks mounted under each wing outboard of the landing gear, and given the designation Hurricane IIB. By the end of 1941 Hurricane IIBs were cleared to carry the more useful 500 pound bomb. Alternatively, Mk IIs were able to carry a 44 (Imperial) gallon fuel tank on the wing hardpoint under each wing, or a 90 (Imperial) gallon fuel tank under each wing for ferry purposes.

Hurricane Mk IIB Hurri-bombers, as they became known, with twelve gun wings were in RAF squadron service by the end of 1940, but it would be the fall of 1941 before they made their first raid on occupied Europe. In the interim, Fighter Command re-built its strength for what would obviously be a protracted period of cross-Channel operations.

Extensive tests were conducted to determined the best method of employing fighter bombers; the Air Fighting Development Unit developed tactics that would become standard operational procedures for Hurri-bomber squadrons. The first Hurri-bomber strike on the continent was made on 30 October 1941 when a pair of No 607 Squadron Hurricane Mk IIBs attacked a transformer station near Tingry. On the 31st it was the turn of the Canadians of No 402 Squadron which dispatched eight Hurri-bombers to bomb the airfield at Berck-sur-Mer with 250 pound bombs.

Hurri-bomber flights usually consisted of aircraft flying in pairs over the Channel at zero feet, climbing to 6,000 ft to cross the French or Belgian coast and then climbing to 18,000 feet to the target. The raiders then dropped to zero feet if the target was buildings. Making a level approach, the Hurricanes pulled up to release their bombs into the buildings, each bomb thus having enough momentum to usually penetrate the walls.

As attacks developed using larger numbers of aircraft, often with accompanying escorts, the Hurricanes would approach a target in sections of four, flying at right angles to the target. The Hurricanes then turned through ninety degrees to make the their attack dive as other sections dived to split the flak defenses. Bombs released from 5,000 to 10,000 feet took some twelve seconds to detonate.

Carrying wing bombs, the Hurricane IIB had approximately the same combat range as a standard fighter — about 150 miles. Most sorties were carried out by daylight but there were some nocturnal outings for Hurri-bombers, particularly over the Dover Straits. In good weather night flying Hurricanes also flew reconnaissance sorties, using flares to guide other aircraft onto worthwhile targets.

In August of 1941 No 81 and 134 Squadrons undertook a unique operation when they were combined to form 151 Fighter Wing and were shipped to Vaenga near Murmansk in the Soviet Union to train Russian pilots and ground crews on Hurricanes. Using tropicalized Hurricane Mk IIBs the wing flew patrols and escort missions for Soviet bombers while instructing their hosts. By November the bulk of the wing's personnel had completed the task of training the initial Red Air Force Hurricane units and prepared to go home. All of the wing's twelve gun fighters were presented to the Russians.

By early 1942 in the European Theater the Hurricane was rapidly being replaced in the day fighter role, the Dieppe raid of 18 August being its last major European operation. Hurricane daylight sorties were increasingly of a secondary nature and by year's end most operational activity conducted by Hurricanes was at night.

(Above) The hazards of air turbulence experienced by a pilot of No 3 Refresher Flying Unit resulted in wing damage to this Hurricane IIB. The aircraft sank during its landing approach, hitting trees, but the pilot got down safely. (Robertson)

(Below) This Gloster-built Hurricane Mk IIB (BE193) seen at Cox's Bazaar during 1943 was flown by F/O Buckland of No 28 Squadron. (Via R L Ward)

(Above) Dispersal scene at Murmansk with a Hurricane Mk IIB belonging to No 134 Squadron nearest the camera. These uniquely-marked RAF fighters carried dual letter/number identity codes on the fuselage for recognition by Russian and British personnel respectively. 'G' was the initial letter of No 134 Squadron, and an 'F' the initial letter of No 82 Squadron, the other half of 151 Wing. (Hawker)

(Above) Major General A A Kuznetsov, Commanding Officer of the Soviet Air Force of the Northern Fleet, about to fly a Hurricane Mk IIB (Z5252) at Murmansk in October of 1941, shortly after the aircraft had been handed over by personnel of No 151 Wing. The lower wing roundels have been overpainted and Red stars have been added.

Hurricane IIA four .303 Brownings

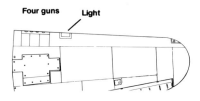

Four guns   Light

(Below Right) Nose-over of a Mk IIB (BG802) at Cox's Bazaar and believed to be another aircraft of No 29 Squadron. A 44 (Imperial) gallon fuel tank is carried under the port wing. (Ward)

Hurricane IIB six .303 Brownings

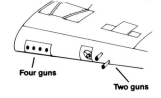

Four guns   Two guns

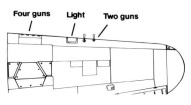

Four guns   Light   Two guns

44 gallon Drop Tank

250 pound Bomb

HURRICANE MK IIC

The origins of the Mk IIC stemmed from Spec F.37/35, which called for a single-seat day and night fighter armed with four 20mm cannon. Hawker proposed a cannon armed version of the Hurricane and while enthusiastic about the far heavier firepower of the cannon, the Air Ministry had reservations about the cannon's effect on the structural integrity of a single engine design. There were also precious few cannon available. Well before the war, Hispano had been approached in regard to obtaining rights to manufacture their excellent 20mm cannon in the UK so that supplies would be secure in case of war. Hispano, however, not wishing to grant a license to a competitor, refused, but set up a UK production facility. However, because of the Air Ministry's reservations about cannon armed single engine aircraft the F.37/35 contract went to Westland to produce the cannon armed twin-engined Whirlwind.

Hawker undertook feasibility testing of a cannon armed Hurricane using a Hurricane Mk I (L1750) fitted with a Swiss 20mm Oerlikon gun in a fairing mounted under each wing. The first flight was made on 24 May 1939, with the aircraft being tested at A&AEE, and operational trials being conducted by No 151 Squadron.

The company then adapted a pair of battle-damaged wings to accept twin internally mounted 20mm Hispano-Suiza cannon in each wing using the existing drum feed, and test flew these on Mk I P2640 on 7 June 1940. Despite some loss of performance, the potential of cannon armament on Hurricanes was proven and additional conversions followed as the cannon supply increased (entirely from Hispano's UK sources). The first converted aircraft was flown on 6 February 1941. The loss of performance found in the Mk I prototype was overcome with the more powerful 1,280 hp Merlin XX engine of the Mk II, four Mk Is (V2461, Z2588, Z2885 and Z2891) serving as prototypes for the production Mk IIC.

While Mk IIC production would run to 4,711 aircraft, the highest production of any Hurricane variant, numerous examples had actually been built as Mk IIAs or IIBs and were redesignated Mk IICs when

(Above) Armed with Hispano No 1 Mk I cannon with recoil spring sleeves, BD867 banks into a strafing run. Powder stains from the guns can be seen coming out of the fairings on the leading edge as well as from the cartridge chutes. (IWM)

(Below) The Mk IIC configured for European operations and unencumbered by the tropical filter was the most aesthetically pleasing of all the Hurricane Marks. QO-Y belonged to No 3 Squadron during 1941. (Hawker)

(Above) This nosed over Mk IIC (BE432), belonging to No 80 Squadron at Sidi Barrani during late 1941, carries the comparatively rare full complement of fuselage code letters in the desert. A Mk IIC, it is serialed BE432. (R L Ward).

Hurricane Mk IIB

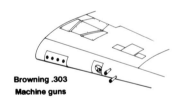
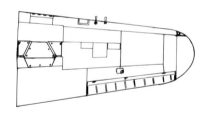

Browning .303
Machine guns

Hurricane Mk IIC

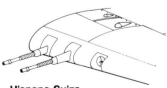
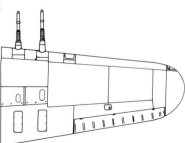

Hispano-Suiza
No 1 Mk I 20mm Cannon

(Above) One of the few squadrons to perpetuate its prewar unit marking on combat aircraft during the war, No 73 Squadron marked both its Hurricane IICs and its Spitfires with the two-tone Blue arrowhead device. BD930 is being loaded onto a Queen Mary for repair after crash landing in the desert. The short ventral fillet suggests the fitting of a belly camera. (IWM)

cannon were retro-fitted. Hawker, Gloster and Austin-Morris built the majority of the Hurricane Mk IICs, others being converted from Canadian examples and re-designated Mk IICs. At least 251 Mk IIB/Cs were built in Canada, with a few further examples being completed within a mixed batch of Mk II/XIs.

The first UK-based Mk IIs were operational in September of 1940 and by October of 1941 fifty-seven home based RAF squadrons were flying Hurricane IIs, typically a mixture of B and C variants. Overseas, there were twenty-five Hurricane squadrons by December of 1941, eighteen of them flying tropicalized Mk IICs. In total, variants of the Mk II would see service with no less than eighty-seven RAF squadrons world-wide.

(Below) Another Mk IIC of No 73 Squadron awaits the attention of the recovery party. The cannon have already been removed and the canopy has been shrouded against the sun. (Shores)

(Above) Tight echelon starboard formation of tropicalized Mk IICs belonging to No 94 Squadron. In the background are the three MacRobert Hurricanes, paid for by Lady MacRobert in memory of her three sons, all killed while flying. From the back they are HL844 'Sir Alasadair'; HL735 'Sir Iain' and HL851 'Sir Roderic'. A fourth aircraft was named appropriately 'The Lady.' (IWM)

(Above) A tropicalized Hurricane Mk IIC (5307) of the SAAF Operational Training Unit at Waterkloof. (Robertson)

(Below) A Mk IIC fitted with two 44 (imperial) gallon drop tanks at Enfiderville, Tunisia on 28 June 1943. (Howard Levy)

(Below) Mk IIC BN162 of No 451 Squadron at Alexandria in April of 1943. (Shores)

(Above) Carrying out night work was No 43 Squadron, which had this presentation Hurricane 'Lothaire' on strength, believed to be at Tangmere in late 1942. The pilot is Sgt E W Bierer. (IWM)

(Below) With its serial repainted under the tailplane, a Hurricane Mk IIC HL864 of No 87 Squadron awaits night duty early in the summer of 1942. The scroll under the cockpit carried a name of one or two words to mark the aircraft's purchase through public donation.

(Above) The 'V for victory' sign is given by James MacLachlan, who lost his left forearm in combat flying from Malta. Back in the UK he commanded No 1 Squadron flying Hurricane Mk IICs on night intruder sorties. He was credited with 16 1/2 victories before dying of wounds later in the war. MacLachlan's personal aircraft, 'JO-Q' is believed to be at Redhill, Surrey, in July of 1941. (IWM)

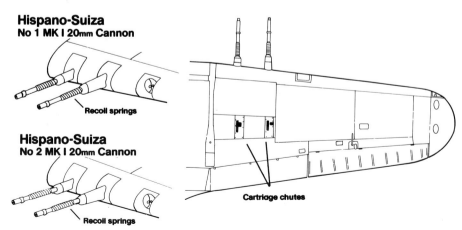

Hispano-Suiza
No 1 MK I 20mm Cannon

Recoil springs

Hispano-Suiza
No 2 MK I 20mm Cannon

Recoil springs

Cartridge chutes

(Above) A Polish pilot in a No 87 Squadron Mk IIC which displays both the unit title and the presentation name 'Agra'. The Hurricane carries a hastily brushed-on coat of Black paint over standard camouflage for night operations. (GSHI)

(Above) Resting on a wheeled dolly to move it down the line, this Mk IIC is having its 20MM Hispano No 2 Mk I cannon installed. On the nearest gun can be seen the gas cylinder above the barrel and the recoil spring of the No 2 Mk I design. The No 1 Mk I cannon fitted to early Mk II Hurricanes had a fairing that covered the rear of the recoil spring. (Hawker)

(Below) Mk IIC of No 247 Squadron with a rather unusual presentation of code letters that this unit carried while on night intruder duties. The aircraft is almost certainly serialed BD836. (IWM)

(Above) A rather knocked — about Hurricane IIC which suffered a wheels-up landing and has been put back on its feet with screw-jacks and oil drums. The composite wooden airscrew blades have shattered. (Ward)

(Above Right) Tropicalized Mk IIC (LB957) of No 34 Squadron in Burma with its SEAC White recognition bands restricted to the fin. (Robertson)

(Below Right) The only Hurricanes to wear D-Day Invasion Stripes were those of second line units likely to visit France on non-operational duties during the weeks following the invasion. This aircraft is having news copy stowed in a fuselage bay. (IWM)

(Below) Presentation Mk IIC 'Bastar' prior to delivery. The single oversize wing blister is unusual. (Hawker)

Foreign Supplied Hurricane MK IIs

The Russians received 2,776 Mk IIs apart from those aircraft left behind by No 151 Wing. Mk IIs supplied to Russia included a number of Mk I airframes brought up to Mk II standards, and some Canadian Mk Xs. The Soviets modified some of their Hurricanes to two-seaters and added rear-firing gun positions to a number of Hurricanes. The most common Russian modification was to reduce the number of guns, fitting two 20MM ShVAK cannon and two 12.7MM UB machine guns. Another modification enabled Hurricanes to use Russian rocket projectiles in the ground-attack role.

Three more squadrons of the South African Air Force, Nos 7, 40 and 43 used Mk IIs in North Africa, as did eight squadrons of the Royal Indian Air Force in the Far East — a theater where the Hurricane was to shoulder the lion's share of fighter duties through the end of the war. In Western Europe the Hurricane's role became increasingly that of a fighter-bomber after the end of 1941, with more potent aircraft taking over the daylight interceptor role, but in the nocturnal intruder role the Hurricane IIC reigned supreme until the introduction of the Mosquito. Among those who used the Hurricane to good effect at night were Czech ace Karel Kuttelwascher and James Maclachlan of No 1 Squadron, and Richard Playne Stevens of No 151 Squadron.

Turkey and Yugoslavia were among the wartime Allied nations to take deliveries of Mk IICs. The Free French operated Mk II squadrons in Syria and the Western Desert in addition to those Free French units flying with the RAF in Europe. The Irish Air Corps received six Mk IICs and Egypt used the Mk II to boost its two defensive squadrons formed on Mk Is. Portugal took delivery of 115 Mk IIs following an agreement with Britain in 1943 granting Allied forces the use of bases in the Azores. The majority of these were IICs, some of which soldiered on into the 1950s. Several returned to the UK to star in the Battle of Britain film *Angels One-Five*, masquerading as Mk Is.

During the last years of the war and immediately afterward Hurricanes were shipped to Persia to complete the order for eighteen aircraft placed in 1939. They included sixteen Hurricane Mk IICs and a two-seat trainer conversion of a Mk IIB (KZ232), which flew with both open and enclosed second cockpits.

When nine years of Hurricane production ended during the week of 6 August 1944, the last off the line was a Mk IIC (PZ865). It, along with a handful of other Hurricanes, survive to the present day.

(Below) The last country to use Hurricanes operationally was Portugal, which did not finally replace them until 1954. This immaculate aircraft was one of 115 Mk IIB and C models delivered to the Portuguese Air Force and was probably part of Esquadrilha de Caca No 1 at Espinho during the late 1940s. Code letters were used on only a few types of aircraft in Portuguese service, 'VX' and 'RV' being also used on Hurricanes. (Hawker)

(Above) A Persian Mk IIC on a pre-delivery flight over England with capped cannon barrel fairings. (Hawker)

(Above) The modified two-seated trainer bound for Persia (Iran) after construction at Kingston. Although the aircraft not did fly with cannon installed — it has the the ammunition bay wing blisters, which were subsequently removed. (Hawker)

(Below) To improve comfort for the student pilot, the Persian two-seater later had a modified Tempest canopy installed. (Hawker)

HURRICANE MK IID

Work on a heavy anti-tank gun for the Hurricane began in 1941, with initial experiments centered around the 40mm Rolls-Royce BF (Belt Feed) gun with twelve rounds, but the production weapon for the Hurricane Mk IID was the 40mm Vickers 'S' gun firing fifteen rounds. Slung in streamlined fairings under each wing, the Vickers cannon were 'ranged' by a pair of .303 Brownings with tracer ammunition.

Removal of all but two of the internally mounted wing machine guns, used for ranging, was necessitated by the weight of the Vickers cannon, a critical factor which also meant that operational Mk IIDs initially carried no armor protection for the pilot, engine or radiator. Consequently, although the Hurricane IID was an extremely potent ground attack aircraft — indeed it was the most accurate anti-tank aircraft the RAF had during World War II — it was vulnerable to defensive fire. Efforts were made to provide the necessary protection, with the addition of 386 pounds of armor plate, but only at a heavy performance penalty with an all up weight of 8,218 pounds.

Operational use of the Hurricane Mk IID was limited to five squadrons, all but one of which were based overseas — Nos 5, 6, 20 and 184 RAF Squadrons and 7 SAAF — only No 184 operated in Europe, and for a short time used armored Mk IIDs in Europe. The other four squadrons were extremely effective in the Middle East from the summer of 1942, when No 6 Squadron received the first Mk IIDs.

(Above) Early trials of the Vickers 'S' guns in 1942 included ground firing with the aircraft jacked up to flying attitude. (Robertson)

(Below) Production Hurricane Mk IIDs were mostly shipped overseas and the majority of both marks were soon fitted with tropical filters. Only No 184 Squadron operated them in Europe. (Robertson)

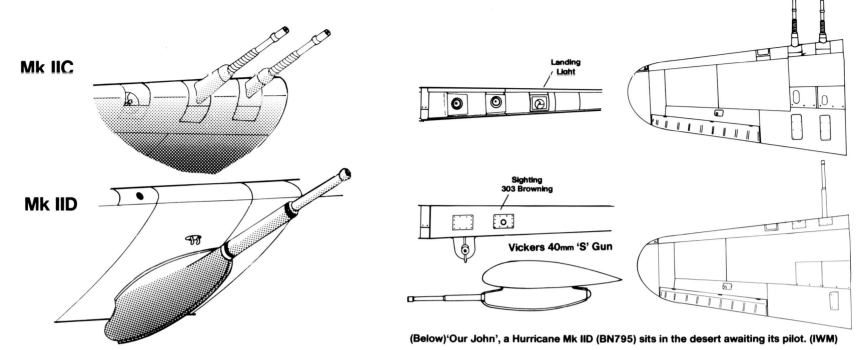

Mk IIC

Mk IID

Landing Light

Sighting 303 Browning

Vickers 40mm 'S' Gun

(Below)'Our John', a Hurricane Mk IID (BN795) sits in the desert awaiting its pilot. (IWM)

HURRICANE MK IIE

The first production Hurricane fitted with Universal wings capable of accommodating the full range of external weapons and fuel tanks was designated the Hurricane Mk IIE. Because of its close support duties the front fuselage was provided with additional armor protection. The Mk IIE prototype (KZ193) first flew on 23 March 1943 powered by a Merlin 27, driving a Rotol R.S.5/11 three bladed propeller. Production aircraft were powered by the Merlin 32 and began rolling out in April of 1943. With the engine change to the Merlin 32 it was decided to provide the variant with its own designation, and after 270 Mk IIEs had been built at Kingston the designation was changed to Hurricane Mk IV.

HURRICANE PR MK II

To provide photo reconnaissance a number of Mk IIs, and Mk Is brought up to Mk II standards with Merlin XX engines, were equipped with cameras. Mk IIA, Mk IIB, and Mk II C wings were usually retained but the armament was removed in order to install extra fuel tanks. Re-engined Mk I airframes were allocated new serial numbers. Three variants were provided: *Tactical-reconnaissance, Fighter-reconnaissance,* and *photographic-reconnaissance*. The tactical-reconnaissance Hurricane was usually equipped with two oblique F.24 cameras with 8 inch lenses mounted in the rear fuselage. The Fighter-reconnaissance variant was usually equipped with a forward facing F.24 or cine camera mounted in the starboard wing root. The Photographic-reconnaissance variant was equipped with three cameras with 14 inch lenses mounted in the rear of the fuselage, and usually operated at above 30,000 feet. The Far East received small numbers of PR Hurricanes with two or three cameras installed. Originally modified by No 2 PRU in the desert, they formed the nucleus of No 5 PRU (later renumbered No 3 PRU) at Rangoon, Burma in 1942. Although the total number of photographic reconnaissance Hurricanes was small, they did sterling work in areas where newer or more suitable aircraft were lacking. The PR Hurricanes' main drawback was lack of range; the Spitfire and other types were more adaptable in this respect and the Hurricane was gradually replaced as more suitable aircraft became available. Other Hurricanes undertook a dual fighter/reconnaissance role, often with reduced armament.

HURRICANE MK IV

There was no Hurricane Mk III although this designation was originally reserved for aircraft powered by American built Packard Merlin engines.

In 1943 the Hurricane Mk IV, the last major production model, appeared. Externally identical to the earlier Mk II series the first example (KX405) flew with a Rotol four-bladed propeller powered by the Merlin 32 engine. Production Mk IVs retained the three-bladed airscrews for either the 1,624 hp Merlin 24 or 27 engines (up-rated tropicalized versions of the Merlin XX engine). Designed specifically for the ground attack role additional armor plate was installed around the belly radiator. Total armor weight was 350 pounds, most of it protecting the pilot and the engine.

The RAF received 524 Hurricane Mk IVs most of which went to the Middle and Far Eastern theaters, although Nos 137, 164 and 184 Squadrons flew the Mk IV variant operationally from UK bases until the type's withdrawal in March of 1944. Three RCAF squadrons, Nos 438, 439 and 440 also flew Hurricane IVs in a non-operational role in England, prior to converting to Typhoons.

Of the units that saw action, only Nos 137 and 164 Squadrons are known to have used their 40MM guns in combat, the majority of sorties being with rocket projectiles. The Mk IV was in action from June of 1943 in northwest Europe, and one of the premier RAF Hurricane units, No 6 Squadron, received its first examples in July while operating from Ben Gardane, Tunisia.

Few details have emerged about the use of the big gun Hurricanes against continental targets. Not the most agile of aircraft while carrying 40MM cannons, Hurricane IV tank busters were given heavy fighter escort. Their targets were mainly trains rather than tanks.

Rocket Projectiles (RP) trials with Hurricanes began as early as October of 1941, when a Mk II

(Above) Hurricane Mk IV (BP173) on a test flight from Langley carrying a full load of 60 pound rocket projectiles (RPs).

(Z2415) flew with three launching rails mounted under each wing. Retaining full gun armament it commenced trials at Boscombe Down early in 1942 and was soon followed by two more Mk IIs (BN583 and BN902), both of which — unlike the first aircraft — were tropicalized.

While aiming the rockets was rudimentary and their accuracy left something to be desired, the RP's destructive power was undisputed and the RAF standardized on three types: a 25 pound solid armor-piercing RP, a 60 pound semi-armor piercing RP and a 25 pound steel practice RP. More widely associated with the Typhoon, rockets were widely used by Hurricanes, and much of the operational testing was carried out by the Hurricane, despite a considerable performance handicap. Not only did the Hurricane have to lift the heavy projectiles, but also eight launching rails and a steel anti-blast plate sandwiched between the rails and the wing. Nevertheless, within limitations RPs were effective against targets in occupied Europe, and in the Balkans and the Far East, RP equipped Hurricanes were excellent ground-attack aircraft. The Mk IV eventually equipped eleven first-line squadrons.

Numerous attacks were made by Hurricanes carrying asymetric loads consisting of a fuel tank under one wing and four RP rails under the other. No 184 Squadron tried carrying rockets under one wing and a 40MM under the other, but the yaw effect created when the cannon was fired was so severe that the rockets and rails broke loose from the wings.

Among the Mk IVs used for trials was KZ706, a late-production machine which tested the Long Tom rocket with a 500 pound warhead. The weapon was launched at the Pendine Sands Range at the end of the war, Hurricane KZ706 carrying one under each wing.

The 40MM cannon and the rocket projectile gave the Hurricane a new lease on life in the Mediterranean and Far Eastern theaters, where until the end of hostilities it remained the only Allied single-engined fighter fitted with the big anti-tank gun. While other fighters, notably the P-51 Mustang carried rockets, their sortie rate with these weapons was limited. No 6 Squadron, the foremost user of the Hurricane in the ground attack role, converted to Mk IVs, beginning RP strikes during the drive through southern Italy. Until joined by No 351 (Yugoslav) Squadron, No 6 Squadron was the only Hurricane IV unit available in Europe.

In both day and night operations, No 6 Squadron devised its own tactics for rocket strikes against a variety of targets. In order to make maximum use of their unguided weapons it was found that a fifteen degree dive, with the aircraft at precisely 225 knots was required. Release point for 60 pound rockets was 300-400 yards from the target and closer (200 yards) when using the 25 pound warhead type for night attacks, preferably in moonlight.

Not only did No 6 Squadron finish out the war with Hurricanes, but continued to fly them for seven-

(Above) A Hurricane Mk IV (HL857) carrying two 44 (Imperial) gallon fuel tanks in service in the Far East. (Ward)

(Below) Armorers trundle rockets to dispersal pans at Prkos for attachment to Hurricane Mk IVs of No 351 Squadron, the second Yugoslavian manned unit in the RAF. The Hurricanes were appropriately marked with Yugoslav Red stars. (Shores)

teen months after the war, mainly on Army co-operation duties. No 6 Squadron flew the last Hurricane sortie in first line service before the Hurricane was officially withdrawn on 15 January 1947.

In the Far East, squadrons became adept at handling their Hurricanes to the detriment of the Japanese. Using both Mk IIs and IVs against armor, soft-skinned vehicles, river traffic and troop concentrations Nos 11, 20, 34, 42, 60 and 113 Squadrons ensured that the enemy had little respite during the final days of the fighting in Burma.

41

(Above) It was not unusual for Mk IVs to carry a drop tank under one wing and rockets under the other wing. This machine had a striking flying devil insignia under the exhaust stacks on the port side and was on strength with No 6 Squadron in the Balkans, probably at Prkos during the spring of 1945. (Shores)

(Above) The rocket/fuel tank loads were able to be carried on either wing, as evidenced by these Mk IVs believed to belong to 6 Squadron at Prkos. (Shores)

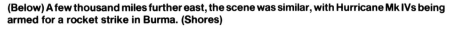

(Below) A few thousand miles further east, the scene was similar, with Hurricane Mk IVs being armed for a rocket strike in Burma. (Shores)

(Below) A Hurricane Mk IV and Spitfire IX of No 1687 Bomber Defense Flight at Scampton in 1944. (Robertson)

HURRICANE MK V

There were only two Hurricane Mk Vs built. Serialled KZ193 and NL255, both were Mk IV conversions based on the 1,700 hp Merlin 32 engine driving a four-bladed propeller. They served as trials aircraft for a possible production variant. The first flight was made on 3 April 1943. Despite a maximum speed of 326 mph determined in Boscombe Down tests with both aircraft being fitted with tropicalization and carrying 40mm cannon, the necessary ground-boosting of the engine showed little practical advantage, especially since the Merlin 32 exhibited overheating and a consequent shortness between overhauls. When testing was finished both machines were returned to standard Mk IV configuration and the project was dropped.

(Below)One of the two Hurricane Mk Vs (KZ193) built. It has a four-bladed Rotol propeller for the Merlin 32 engine and twin 40mm anti-tank cannon. Since the Merlin 32, boosted for take to 1,700 hp, offered little practical advantage over the 1,624 hp Merlin 32 of the Mk IV, and experienced considerable overheating problems, the Mk V project was abandoned. (Hawker)

43

HURRICANE MK X

By the time war broke out, the Royal Canadian Air Force (RCAF) had nineteen Hurricane Mk Is on strength, these having been the subject of an order (for twenty) placed before hostilities commenced. After negotiations a further Mk I (L1848) was sent by Hawker Aircraft to Canadian Car & Foundry (CC&F) along with complete plans on microfilm for production of Hurricane Mk Is powered by British Merlin III engines shipped from England to Canada.

Since the Hurricane Mk I was likely to continue development, Hawker requested that an adequate gap in Mark Numbers be left to allow for further British designations, and consequently CC&F produced Hurricanes beginning with the Mark X designation. Canadian production went so well that the first Canadian produced Hurricane Mk I was delivered only a year after the pattern aircraft was shipped. After 166 Merlin III powered Hurricanes were produced, production was switched to the Mk X, the designation used to identify Hurricanes powered by the American manufactured Packard Merlin 28 powerplant. All 434 Hurricane Mk Is were built to British contracts, with twenty-five being taken over by the RCAF, and given Canadian serials. All aircraft were produced with eight gun armament, although in numerous cases this was changed to twelve machine guns or four cannon for trans-shipment to other theaters or to the Russians. One Mk X, RCAF 1362 (AG310) was experimentally fitted with a fixed ski landing gear incorporating hydraulic trimming.

(Above) Canadian Hurricane Mk X in overall Aluminum finish with a Red and Blue bordered tail band and a black anti-glare panel. An ex-RAF tropicalized Middle East machine, it was passed to the SAAF Central Flying School at Norton, Southern Rhodesia. (Robertson)

HURRICANE MK XI

Essentially similar to the Mk X, the Hurricane Mk XI designation was applied to aircraft fitted with RCAF equipment built in a batch of fifty that were mixed in with Mk IIs on UK contracts. A further sub-variant, the Hurricane Mk XIB is believed to have referred to installation of the Packard-Merlin 29 engine with a different gear reduction ratio.

(Above) An RCAF Hurricane Mk XII (5584) of No 163 Squadron at Sea Island, Vancouver in June of 1943. The protruding gun muzzles were typical of some Canadian-built Hurricanes. (Robertson)

(Below) A leaping bison badge adorns this RCAF Hurricane Mk XII (5470) of No 1 OTU at Bagotville, Quebec. Canadian-based Hurricanes often flew without spinners. 31 July 1943. (RCAF)

HURRICANE MK XII

Initially designated the Hurricane Mk IIB (Can), the 474 Hurricane Mk XIIs produced were powered by Packard Merlin 29 engines. Serving entirely with Canadian fighter units, they carried serial numbers RCAF 5376-5775, and equipped ten fighter squadrons in Canada. They were used in both fighter and army co-operation roles, primarily to maintain Canada's security in the event of a determined enemy attack on her shipping. Hurricane Mk XIIs along with other aircraft flew continuous offshore patrols, on watch for German U-boats, but no contact was recorded.

A Hurricane Mk XII (RCAF 5624) was the second Hurricane to be converted to take a ski landing gear and was tested at Rockcliffe early in 1943. Even though a speed restriction to 300 mph was recommended, the ski gear worked adequately but no operational flights were made. This particular Mk XII, in common with the majority of Hurricanes flown by the RCAF in Canada, did not have a spinner over the airscrew hub.

Including the Sea Hurricane XIIA, Canadian Car and Foundry built 1,451 Hurricanes, with production terminating during the summer of 1943. CC&F also turned out 1,206 Hurricane wings and 1,168 oleo legs under one of the most successful early programs for the Canadian aviation industry.

SEA HURRICANE MK I

Three Royal Navy squadrons, Nos 803, 807 and 811, used Hurricane fighters which were indistinguishable from RAF Mk Is. They were identified in records as Sea Hurricane Mk Is — or merely as Sea Hurricanes — to denote their Royal Navy ownership. Of the trio, only 803 Squadron used these early aircraft operationally when it was equipped with the ex-RAF machines at Dekheila, Egypt in May of 1941. In June the squadron moved to Palestine, beginning shore-based operations against Syria. In August 803 Squadron became part of the Royal Navy Fighter Squadron, a combined unit in the Western Desert, until moving to the Far East in 1942.

SEA HURRICANE MK IA

With the loss of two British aircraft carriers, COURAGEOUS and GLORIOUS, coupled with an alarming increase in shipping losses, in October of 1940 the Directorate of Research and Development requested that Hawker investigate the possibility of the Hurricane being equipped with spools and hardware for catapult launchings. Hawker informed the Directorate that a prototype could be ready in five weeks. On 19 January of 1941 twenty catapult spools and modification kits were ordered. Two weeks later an additional thirty modification kits were ordered.

Entering service during the early spring of 1941, the first navalized Hurricanes were conversions of ex-RAF Mk Is for catapult launching from the bows of merchant freighters and naval vessels to provide convoy protection from long range air attack when aircraft carrier support was not available. The majority of the fifty examples were used by the Merchant Ship Fighter Unit, and initially manned by volunteer Fleet Air Arm (FAA) personnel who were replaced by RAF personnel as soon as their training was completed. To withstand the shock of a catapult launch, in which the Hurricane was accelerated to a flying speed of sixty knots in eighty feet using a bank of two inch rockets, the Hurricane had the fuselage strengthened and wing and fuselage attachment points installed for catapult spools, as well as eye-bolts to lash the Sea Hurricanes down in heavy seas.

Although early catapult tests were with the landing gear down, Hurricanes mounted on ships for operational sorties kept their mainwheels retracted — there was little need for landing gear, since the sorties were strictly one-way trips — the pilot being obliged to ditch his aircraft and take to his dinghy, since there was usually no place to land. Hopefully the pilot was rescued by a ship in the convoy. During the Fall of 1941 Sea Hurricanes received the addition of 44 gallon auxiliary fuel tanks providing the pilot with additional range increasing the possibility of reaching land.

A total of fifty British ships were equipped with fighter catapults (principally Hurricanes but also Fairey Fulmars), there being thirty-five freighters known as Catapult Aircraft Merchantmen (CAM-ships), and five Naval Fighter Catapult Ships (FCS). One of the latter, HMS MAPLIN, the only RN vessel to actually carry a Hurricane into action and the first to launch her aircraft in anger. On 18 June 1941 MAPLIN was part of a convoy being shadowed by a four engine Focke-Wulf Fw 200 Condor and shot it down.

The first merchant ship catapult launch took place on 1 November 1941 when the EMPIRE FOAM's Hurricane chased off a prowling Fw-200 Condor. Further successes were to follow over the next eighteen months. In February of 1942 MAPLIN's complement of Hurricanes was increased from two to three and she remained the sole FCS on operations until reconversion in June of 1942.

Replenishment of aircraft was necessary if the CAM-ship had launched its fighter en route prior to reaching port at the other end of a convoy escort duty. Therefore Sea Hurricanes were located at the opposite end of the supply routes from Britain in Canada, Gibraltar and Murmansk in Russia, with the UK ports of Belfast, Merseyside, Bristol and Clydeside being the UK landing points.

As the fighter catapult escort ships entered their first full year of war service, modifications were made to the Sea Hurricane to improve the pilots' chances in the event of a ditching. An improved method of jettisoning the sliding cockpit hood was introduced in 1942, as was the Type K inflatable single-seat dinghy. In its Mk II version, this was stowed as a seat pack with the parachute, an arrangement specially for the Hurricane. A further aid for a pilot operating over Arctic waters was the installation of a socket for electrical supply to heated boots and gloves, and a cockpit heater.

Even though the score of the Hurricats, as the catapult Sea Hurricane was called, was small, their very presence probably saved numerous ships from attack. From November of 1941 to July of 1943,

seven German aircraft were shot down and four damaged for the loss of two pilots, by both naval and merchant vessels carrying fighters.

A further fifty Mk I Hurricanes from Canadian production were earmarked for conversion to catapult launched Sea Hurricanes, although the majority of these were operated from shore bases by a total of nine FAA squadrons, primarily in the training role. Among these units was 804 Squadron which from May 1941 provided Sea Hurricane Mk IAs for the CAM ships, a task it undertook until the spring of 1942 when this duty was assumed by the RAF's Merchant Ship Fighter Unit.

(Above) A CAM Hurricane mounted on its rocket-assisted catapult. (Robertson)

(Below) Hurricanes being barged to ships fitted with bow catapults during the CAM fighter defense program. Most machines of this Fighter Command unit carried the code 'LU' as carried on this Hurricane Mk I (Z4867), although Hurricanes coded 'KE' and 'NJ' were used in trials and were probably ex-RAF squadron aircraft prior to being repainted. (Robertson)

SEA HURRICANE MK IB

When fitted with a V-frame arrester hood — and appropriately known as the Hooked Hurricane for a time, the Sea Hurricane IB was the first British single seat monoplane fighter to officially operate from a carrier deck. Unofficially the first Hurricanes to land on a carrier were the Hurricane Mk Is of No 46 Squadron RAF, which flew onto HMS GLORIOUS during the ill-fated Norwegian campaign in 1940.

With standard machine gun armament the Mk IB — and all other Sea Hurricanes — did not have wing folding capability. This had been investigated in 1940, but was not proceded with, the result being that most Sea Hurricanes spent their time out in the open sea weather when operating from smaller escort carriers. Despite this Handicap the Sea Hurricane Mk IB performed remarkably well, providing the Royal Navy with a modern fighter capability when the need was paramount.

The Sea Hurricane Mk IB designation was reserved for carrier-borne Sea Hurricanes to distinguish them from the Mk IA Hurricats intended for freighter catapults. Along with an arrester hook, the aircraft was fitted with a release gear, and retaining springs to cushion the shock of an arrested landing and to prevent the hook from bouncing up and striking the underside of the fuselage. When the hook was at a third or more of its travel a green light came on in the cockpit to tell the pilot he could make the landing. Then with considerable skill — and a degree of luck — the hook would catch on one of the deck wires.

Flying from both the armored fleet carriers and the smaller escort carriers, the Sea Hurricane IB equipped thirty-two Fleet Air Arm (FAA) squadrons and was the most widely used version of the Hurricane in the Royal Navy. Highlights of its distinguished naval career were the Atlantic and Russian convoys and the epic runs to Malta, primarily to deliver vital fighters for the Mediterranean island's defense.

Arresting Hook

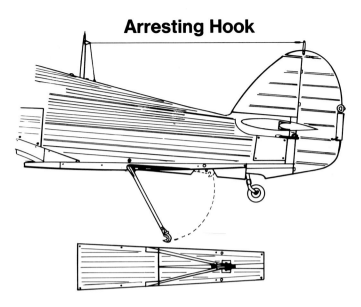

(Below) Sea Hurricane Mk IB being refueled aboard the carrier HMS ARGUS.

SEA HURRICANE MK IIB

Enough strengthened wing Sea Hurricane Mk IIBs were acquired by the FAA to equip six squadrons, the total including some Canadian production MK IIs with twelve gun wings. Users of these latter aircraft included No 800 Squadron operating from HMS BITER during OPERATION TORCH landings in North Africa in November of 1942.

(Above Right) Sea Hurricane IIB in the 'JS' serial range aboard HMS Biter for the TORCH landings in North Africa in November of 1942. An aircraft belonging to 800 Squadron of the FAA, like the majority of British naval aircraft involved in the landings it was marked with US star insignias to give the impression that the operation was all American. The aircraft was flown by 800 Squadron's CO, Lt Cdr J M Bruen. (Via Shores)

(Below) This Canadian built Sea Hurricane IIB (JS327) with twelve gun wings was involved in the Torch landings, and had to make an emergency landing in the beachhead area. (Via Shores)

SEA HURRICANE MK IIC

Trials with Mk II BD878 led to the introduction of a navalized Hurricane Mk IIC variant with cannon armament in May of 1942. Naval radio equipment and arrester hooks were fitted to eighty-one examples converted by General Aircraft, and by July of that year the Fleet Air Arm had about 600 Hurricanes of all marks on strength, some 200 of which were available to operational fleet fighter squadrons, and eighty in use at shore stations, with the rest in reserve.

With the Merlin XX engine, the Sea Hurricane Mk IIC served a total of eighteen FAA squadrons, the type becoming the last to operate from carriers in the hands of Nos 825 and 835 Squadrons on the carriers HMS VINDEX and NAIRANA respectively. Flying on North Atlantic patrols, these aircraft were standard navalized cannon-armed machines, although a few Mk IICs were also equipped with the rocket rails developed for the Mk IV, having their cannon deleted.

SEA HURRICANE MK XIIA

The last Hurricane designation was applied to fifty conversions of the Canadian Mk XII powered by 1,300 hp Packard Merlin 29 engines. Apparently assigned to the RCAF, it is believed that the majority were re-designated by the Royal Navy which received some, and by the Canadian Air Force. No Sea Hurricanes are known to have been operated by the Canadian Navy as such, although some Mk XIIAs are believed to have been used for deck landing training at shore stations.

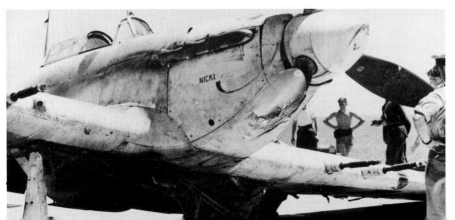

(Above) 'NICKI' A Sea Hurricane Mk IIC (NF700) of No 835 Squadron (FAA) on the deck of HMS Nairana during the summer of 1944. (Ward)

(Above Left) Partially painted invasion stripes are carried on this Sea Hurricane Mk IIC of No 835 Squadron, during the latter half of 1944. (Ward)

(Below Left) 'NICKI' tangled up in deck landing wires after finally coming to a stop on the deck of HMS Nairana in June of 1944. The aircraft, in a predominately White finish, was serialed NF672. (Ward)

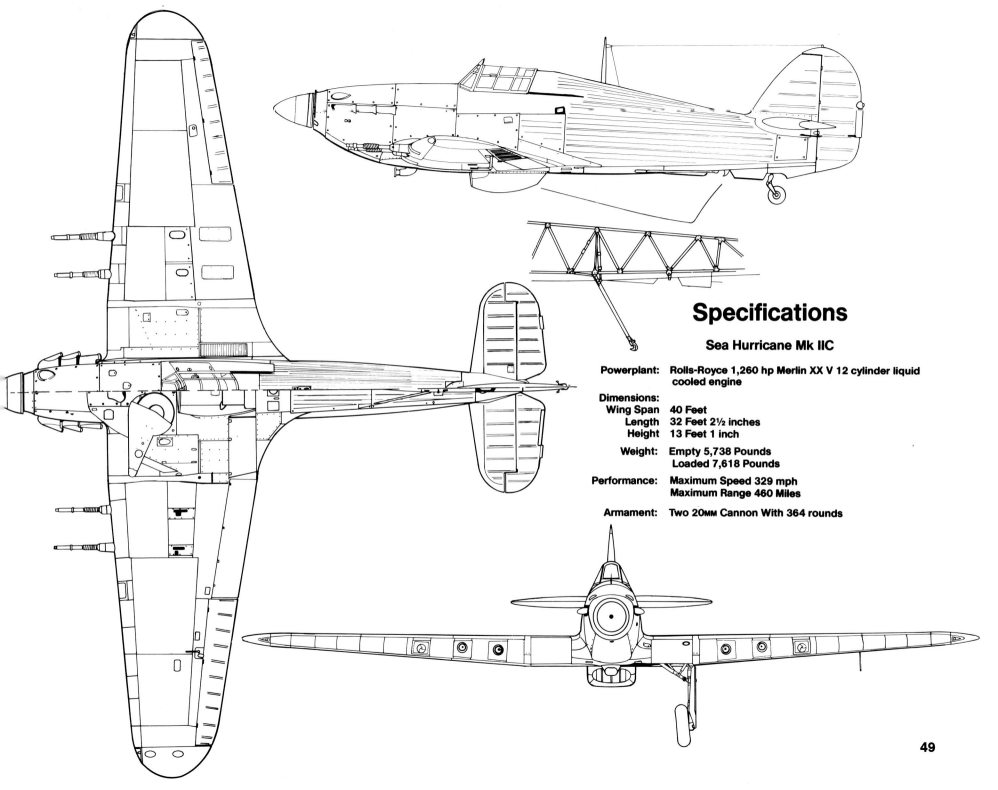

Specifications

Sea Hurricane Mk IIC

Powerplant:	Rolls-Royce 1,260 hp Merlin XX V 12 cylinder liquid cooled engine
Dimensions:	
Wing Span	40 Feet
Length	32 Feet 2½ inches
Height	13 Feet 1 inch
Weight:	Empty 5,738 Pounds
	Loaded 7,618 Pounds
Performance:	Maximum Speed 329 mph
	Maximum Range 460 Miles
Armament:	Two 20ᴍᴍ Cannon With 364 rounds

(Above) The last Hurricane built (PZ865) on a test flight with George Bulman at the controls during the later summer of 1944. Not issued to the RAF during the war, 'The Last of the Many' was retained by Hawker Aircraft, and was later civil-registered and subsequently returned to military colors to join the RAF Battle of Britain Memorial Flight. (Hawker)

(Above) Another survivor (LF363) was delivered to the RAF in January of 1944 and served with No 309 Squadron. After a spell at an Operational Training Unit it led many annual Battle of Britain commemorative fly-pasts before it too became a permanent part of the Memorial Flight. It is seen here after the war at Langley in the company of Iraqi Furies, Sea Furies and an Avro Tudor IV airliner. (Hawker)

(Below) The two Hurricane veterans flying together with a Spitfire in the background in November of 1973. LF363 bears Douglas Bader's personal markings at the time he commanded No 242 Squadron, while PZ865 carries the markings of Squadron Leader Stanford Tuck's Mk I (V6962) of No 257 Squadron. (MoD)

(Below) One of the Hurricanes used in the 'Battle of Britain' film, readily identifiable by the false code letters and the sprayed-on cordite streaks!